FOOD & FEASTS

BETWEEN THE
TWO WORLD WARS

Le migliori paste alimentari

Philip Steele

Wayland

FOOD & FEASTS

Titles in the series

A ZOË BOOK

© 1994 Zoë Books Limited

Devised and produced by
Zoë Books Limited
15 Worthy Lane
Winchester
Hampshire SO23 7AB
England

First published in Great Britain in 1994 by
Wayland (Publishers) Ltd
61 Western Road, Hove
East Sussex BN3 1JD

British Library Cataloguing in Publication Data

Steele, Philip
    Food and Feasts Between the Two World Wars
    I. Title
    641.300941

ISBN 0-7502-1029-X

Printed in Belgium by Proost N.V.
Design: Jan Sterling, Sterling Associates
Picture research: Victoria Sturgess
Production: Grahame Griffiths

Photographic acknowledgments

The publishers wish to acknowledge, with thanks, the
following photographic sources:

Bauhaus-Archiv 17t,19t; The Bridgeman Art Library
6t/City Museum & Art Gallery, Stoke-on-Trent 10t;
Coo-ee Historical Picture Library 14b,16br,22t; Mary
Evans Picture Library title page,3,7t,11tr,16bl,18b,21b,
22b; Robin Garton Gallery, Devizes 6b; H.J.Heinz Ltd 14t;
Hulton Deutsch Collection 4,5t,10b,11tl,13t,18tr,21t;
Kobal Collection 5bl (United Artists), 5br (Paramount),
19b; Peter Newark's Western Americana 7b,9t,11b,12,
18tl,20t&c,24c; Robert Opie Collection 10c,15b,17b,
23t&b,24t; Popperfoto 9b,21c; Topham Picture Source
13b,15t,16t,24b,25; Towner Art Gallery & Local History
Museum, Eastbourne 8t; University of Reading, Rural
History Centre 8b

Cover: Mary Evans Picture Library centre; Topham
Picture Source bottom left.

The publishers have made every effort to trace the
copyright holders, but if they have inadvertently
overlooked any, they will be pleased to make the
necessary arrangement at the first opportunity.

Contents

Introduction

These British children are being given a tea party in the street to celebrate the end of the First World War.

At 11 o'clock on the morning of 11 November 1918, the big guns fell silent on the muddy battlefields of Europe. The First World War had come to an end. Since its start in 1914 this terrible conflict had spread far beyond Europe. It had involved armies from Asia, Australasia, Africa and North America. Nearly ten million young people had been killed.

This war had been called 'the war to end wars'. Everyone was longing for peace, but it was not to be. In the following years there was fighting in Russia, China, Ireland and Spain. And then, once again, war spread like wildfire around the whole world. The Second World War, which lasted from 1939 until 1945, was to be the bloodiest in history.

To those who enjoyed the brief peace, the years between the two world wars were unforgettable. During the 1920s and 30s some of the strict social rules of the pre-war period were laid aside. Fashions were freer and easier.

▷ After Germany's defeat in the First World War, life there was hard. In June 1923 a pound of butter cost up to 13 600 marks. By November of that year there were 4 200 000 000 marks to one US dollar! Shopkeepers had to keep large chests of banknotes by the counter.

▽ Charlie Chaplin sits down to eat his boot for dinner, in a 1925 film called *The Gold Rush*. The American film industry, based in Hollywood, helped people to smile through hard times.

In North America, Europe and Australia young people danced to wild jazz music. During the war, women had worked in factories and on farms, carrying out many of the jobs usually done by men. This helped them to gain more political power. In 1918 British women over thirty gained the vote and in 1928 this was extended to all British women. From 1920 onwards American women could vote in federal elections.

The world was becoming a smaller place, thanks to air travel and the first cheap cars. The radio and the cinema were bringing glimpses of the outside world into many remote country areas.

For thousands of people these were years of great hardship. Large numbers of workers became jobless and their families went hungry. Never had farming and food production been more important. There were great changes in the types of food that people ate. The shops where food was bought changed too.

▽ The popular cartoon sailor, Popeye, urged people to eat spinach. Most western diets were full of fat, sugar and starch. Only a few people were vegetarians. They included the Irish writer George Bernard Shaw, the Indian freedom campaigner Mohandas K Gandhi, and the leader of the German 'Nazis', Adolf Hitler.

Country and crops

▷ The everyday diet of poorer farm workers offered little nourishment. In some parts of the world it was made up mostly of bread, with a main weekly meal of bacon or mutton stew. In other parts of the world the everyday diet might be based on rice, pasta, potatoes or corn meal.

Imagine a small country kitchen in the year 1919. It would have varied greatly from one part of the world to another, but in western countries many things would have been similar. Food would be cooked over a wood-burning stove or a **kitchen range**. Water still probably came from a well or a **pump** in the yard. Above the wooden shelves or **dresser**

◁ In this English cottage in 1929 the kitchen has no gas or electricity and water is still drawn from a well. The floor is paved with stone.

The Women's Institute was started in Canada in 1897. In the years between the wars the same idea was taken up in other countries around the world. Country women would meet regularly and exchange ideas about house-keeping, cooking and preserving food. In those days it was almost unheard of for men to do any cooking in the home.

there might have been a shotgun, used for killing rabbits or ducks.

Much of the food laid out on the wooden table would be produced at home, on the nearest farm or in the village. Milk would probably not be treated, or **pasteurised**. Butter and bread were home-made. Bacon or ham would be home-**cured** and vegetables were grown in the garden.

Some goods, such as sugar, coffee or tea, would have been bought at the village shop or nearest store. Already there were packaged and tinned goods and well-known **brand names**. However, many dry goods were still sold loose. They were measured out, weighed and wrapped in brown paper parcels or bags.

By the year 1939, the same kitchen might have looked rather different. During the previous 20 years many country areas had been connected to piped water and electricity supplies. In place of the old wood stove or range, there might be a new gas or electric cooker.

By now less of the produce on the table would be home-made. Country people were eating more ready-prepared foods from the cities. Over the following 50 years this happened more and more, so that today there is little difference between a town and a country diet.

△ A French cookery book tells its readers how to preserve food. In the 1920s many people bottled their own fruit and vegetables.

▷ Almost everything could be bought in this American general store, in Moundville, Alabama, USA – from soap to candles, biscuits and cheese to mousetraps!

Special occasions

Traditional feasts and festivals provided a rare chance for poorer country families to eat and drink too much! There were Thanksgiving celebrations and barn dances in the United States, Christmas dinners and harvest suppers in Britain, wedding feasts and village festivals in most parts of the world.

▷ In many areas farming continued as it had done for centuries. Power for ploughing was provided by horse or ox. This painting shows horses ploughing a field near Wilmington, in the south of England, in 1917.

Although country people used more home-made and locally produced foods than we do today, farming was already being organized on national and international lines.

The grasslands or **prairies** of Canada and the United States were the bread basket of a whole continent. Vast cattle ranches supplied the **stockyards** of Chicago in the United States and Buenos Aires in Argentina. Huge sheep farms in Australia and New Zealand sent, or **exported**, frozen lamb to the other side of the world to be sold. **Refrigerated transport**, developed in the 1880s, was now common, although aircraft were not yet used for food **freight**.

▽ The first tractors had wheels with metal ridges or spikes. Rubber tyres were first fitted to tractors in 1932.

Farming on this scale was made possible by new technology. The piping of water to country areas made it possible to grow more crops. Lorries and pick-up trucks began to be used on the farms. Tractors began to take the place of horses in some countries. Tractors had been produced in

The 'GLASGOW' *Farm Tractor*

▷ An American farming family of the 1930s takes to the road. Farming life was hard. Many workers had to travel in search of work, which was often seasonal. New farm machinery and economic problems meant that there were fewer and fewer jobs. Trades unions were formed to protect working conditions.

▽ The Communist government of the Soviet Union took control of farming and food production in the 1920s. Small farms were forced to join together, forming 'collective' farms. There were also large farms owned by the state. These workers are on a collective farm near Kharkov, in the Ukraine.

the USA since 1916, and already by 1920 there were 246 000 on American farms. By 1940 there were more than six times as many.

Horses or tractors were used to haul the first clumsy **combine harvesters**, and by 1938 the first motor combines were to be seen in the United States.

Who owned the big farms? In the Americas, wealthy ranchers controlled huge areas of land. In Britain or eastern Germany large estates were still owned by aristocratic families. Middle-sized farms might be farmed by the owner or rented out to a tenant. In the United States it was common for tenants to pay a share of the crop as rent. They were known as **sharecroppers**. Peasant **smallholdings** were still common in many regions, including southern France and Italy. In parts of the world such as India and Africa, most farming continued as it had done for thousands of years.

▷ Horse-drawn carts and wagons were used to transport wood, hay and vegetable crops.

△ Water piped into dry regions of the United States and Australia made fruit-growing possible on a large scale. This grapefruit wrapper came from California.

The crops produced around the world in the 1920s and 30s were much the same as the ones we know today. Wheat, barley, rye, oats, maize and rice were the main **cereal** crops. The potato was the chief root crop in colder lands, while sweet potatoes, yam and cassava were grown in warm regions. Some crops were becoming much more widely grown. Beet was being cultivated for sugar and soya bean for vegetable oil.

The **yield** from the crops planted then was much smaller than it is in the 1990s, now that new, improved types, or **strains**, of plant have been bred. However, science was already playing a greater part in farming, or agriculture. New chemical **fertilizers** were sold from 1926 onwards. They contained a mixture of nitrogen, phosphate and potash.

▽ Milking machines had been invented before the First World War, but it was a long time before they were widely used. They could milk 25 cows in an hour. Cattle were given far fewer drugs than today, and on small farms they were known by names rather than numbers.

△ During the 1920s farmers first tried raising chickens as if they were in a factory rather than a farm. This led to cheaper eggs and 'broiler' birds, but the chickens suffered as a result.

△ North Sea herrings are brought ashore, cleaned and packed in barrels. This scene was painted at the English port of Yarmouth in 1921.

Pests posed a serious problem for farmers. As more and more crops were transported around the world, so were the harmful insects that fed on them. The yellow-and-black striped Colorado beetle originally came from the western United States. It fed on a wild plant called buffalo burr, but soon spread to potato plants. The pest raged eastwards across America. In the 1920s it crossed the Atlantic Ocean in cargo ships and arrived in France, where it devastated potato crops.

Pesticides were used more often. They were first sprayed from aircraft during the early 1920s, but this was still unusual. Some pesticides were very poisonous and were harmful to wildlife. One, called DDT (short for dichloro-diphenyl-trichloroethane), was developed in Switzerland in 1939. Today its use is banned in many countries.

▽ No harvest in 1936, as farm machinery lies buried in the dust of South Dakota, USA.

Crops bite the dust

In the United States large areas of land had been over-farmed. Springs had been tapped and exhausted for water supplies. Trees and grassland had been dug up. The soil soon turned into worthless dust. High winds whipped up the dust and carried it across the continent. Between 1933 and 1937 the Great Plains were stripped of their soil and became little more than a desert – a 'dustbowl'.

△ Hard times for the family of a migrant farmworker. This photograph was taken outside their shack in Amarillo, in the American state of Texas.

This song was sung in the United States in the 1930s. The word 'Hooverize' came from a politician called Herbert Hoover. During the First World War he had told people to eat every scrap of food on their plate.

Beans, bacon and gravy. . .

I was born long ago, in 1894,
And I've seen many a panic, I will own.
I've been hungry, I've been cold,
And now I'm growing old,
But the worst I've seen is 1931.

Oh, those beans, bacon and gravy,
They almost drive me crazy.
I eat them till I see them in my dreams.
When I wake up in the morning
    and another day is dawning,
Yes, I know I'll have another mess of
    beans.

We have Hooverized on butter,
For milk we've only water,
And I haven't seen a steak in many a day,
As for pies, cakes and jellies,
We substitute sowbellies,
For which we work the country roads
    each day.

The years between the wars were ones of extreme wealth and extreme poverty, side by side. This was true in the countryside as well as in the towns.

The contrast was greatest in Africa and Asia, where people from Europe had set up farms, or plantations, to grow crops such as tea or coffee. These settlers were called **colonists**. Local people were paid very little – to work on land which once was theirs.

Even within the world's richer nations there were great differences between the country rich and the country poor. In the United States the **migrant farmworkers** of the dustbowl some-times had to live by trapping birds or stealing food and scraps. They were moved on by the big landowners, who did not want them on their land.

In Britain, the **poacher** was often a local hero. By night he would slip onto the estates of a large landowner and steal salmon from the rivers and hares or game birds from the woods.

In some parts of the world, such as China and the Soviet Union, social unrest, war and

By 1926 more than a third of the world and its peoples were ruled by European countries. The colonists brought in their own farming methods and exported food. They profited from the land while local people often went hungry. In 1930 the Indian freedom campaigner, Mohandas K Gandhi, marched to protest against a law which said that only the British were allowed to manufacture salt in his country.

natural disasters caused starvation, or **famine**. In the winter of 1921-22, about five million Russian peasants died of hunger in the countryside around the River Volga.

Of course, not everyone was very poor or very rich. Many farmers and other country people ate modestly or well and enjoyed a healthy diet.

In Europe, wealthy people would have weekend shooting parties on large country estates. These foreign diplomats were invited to the French president's castle at Rambouillet. The photograph shows the 495 pheasants and 167 rabbits that they have shot.

Cities and suburbs

◁ In the 1920s the yard of the Heinz factory at Harlesden, near London, was stacked with wooden barrels. They contained vegetables preserved in brine. Heinz, a firm founded in the United States, made pickles, sauces, baked beans and ketchup.

Cities now played as important a part in producing food as the countryside. Food processing had become an industry. Foods were cooked, pickled, canned or bottled in large factories. These were often sited in the built-up areas around large cities, or suburbs. Motor and rail transport allowed goods to be delivered direct to shops and stores nationwide.

During the 1920s and 30s processed foods became very popular. These included breakfast cereals such as shredded wheat and cornflakes, cheese portions, fish pastes, sauces, ketchups and salad creams. Many of these foods were designed to save time in preparation. Coffee could be made from concentrated liquid, or **essence**. Powdered instant coffee was

▷ By 1933, factory methods were used in the grading and packing of apples. A conveyor belt was in use at Karragullen, near Perth in Western Australia.

▽ Shopping in an American supermarket in 1949.

introduced during the 1930s. Powdered custards and **blancmanges** provided a cheap and quick dessert.

Some processed foods were made from chemicals rather than natural products. This type of food is called synthetic. Margarine, invented in France in 1869, was now widely used as a cheap substitute for butter. Packaged frozen foods were, as yet, rarely seen in the shops. They were first sold to the public in 1930, at Springfield in the North American state of Massachusetts.

While many people still shopped at street markets and small corner shops, chains of food stores were beginning to appear in the towns. In these stores the food was piled high on the counters and the walls were tiled so that they were easier to keep clean. Much food was still sold loose. Bacon was sliced to order and meats were weighed out. Staff wore starched white aprons.

Supermarket starters

'I could afford to sell a can of milk at cost if I could sell a can of peas and make 2 cents,' said Michael 'King' Cullen, American supermarket pioneer. Early self-service stores included Big Bear and Albers Super Markets Inc. Supermarkets were an all-American invention and were not seen in Europe until the 1950s. And who invented the shopping trolley? S N Goldman, for a US company called Humpty Dumpty Inc, in 1936.

BLUE BAND
Versch Gekarnd

◁ This Dutch advertisement was for a brand of margarine. Advertising played a more and more important part in selling food. Famous brand names appeared in magazines, on street hoardings and on the sides of buses. Food companies sponsored music and comedy programmes on American and European radio stations.

Firsts in the kitchen

1923 Electric refrigerator (Sweden)

1926 Electric kettle (Britain)

1927 Pop-up electric toaster (USA)

1931 Food-mixer with built-in motor (USA)

1936 Food processor (USA)

◁ In city slums the kitchens were often crowded and unhygienic. In many areas, water still had to be collected from a pump or an outside tap. These women chat at the pump in London's East End, in 1933.

▽ A French cookery book shows a kitchen-maid, in neat uniform and cap, preparing the 'starters' for a family meal.

Food was delivered from the stores to the private homes of customers by horse and cart, bicycle or motor van. Other produce was also delivered, such as milk from dairies. This was sometimes ladled directly out of the metal churn rather than being sold in bottles or cartons. In the United States, ice was delivered to homes to keep food cool.

In the wealthier countries, large town houses were run by servants. There were kitchen maids and cooks and butlers to do all the daily chores. They often lived in the house, working 'below stairs' in the basement kitchens. Even middle class families would have a maid or a cook. The servants' lives were often hard and they were poorly paid. In 1939 an experienced cook in London earned about £80 a year.

However, times were changing. Rich people began to employ fewer servants. New, labour-saving inventions made kitchen

▽ Milk is delivered to the home near Perth, Australia, in 1933.

work much easier. **Stainless steel** had been invented in 1913. This meant that less time was spent cleaning and polishing knives and forks. It was many years before all the inventions were widely used, but already they were changing people's ideas about cooking.

In towns and the new suburbs which were growing up, many houses were connected to a gas supply. Gas cookers were at first more popular than electric ones. Refrigerators gradually caught on, but in most houses people still stored food in **pantries** or **larders**. In these small rooms the food could be kept on cool slate or marble slabs. Meat was stored in a **safe**, a small cupboard with a wire mesh door to keep out flies.

△ This kitchen, designed in Germany in 1923, was ahead of its time. It has the trim cupboards and work surfaces we expect in today's kitchens. Most kitchens between the wars were more cluttered.

▷ A new cooker and a neat kitchen became the dream of everyone buying a new home in the middle class suburbs. Women were normally expected to do all the work in the kitchen. Most men did little more than carve the meat at mealtimes.

Meals are always ready to time with a

MAIN

GAS COOKER

△ An unemployed worker sells apples in New York, in about 1931.

△ Bread, margarine and tea were a major part of the diet for poor British families. This may well have been the main meal of the week.

▽ Cooking was easier to control and cleaner with modern cookers. This advertisement appeared in 1938.

Many poor children were given free meals by charities. In Britain they might have received:
○ A breakfast of thin porridge and one slice of bread.
○ A lunch of boiled potatoes and minced meat.
○ One orange or apple twice a week.

The meals that people ate between the wars varied greatly from one country to another. They varied even more from one social class to another.

What was eaten for breakfast, the first meal of the day? In Britain and North America, for poor people, it might be a slice of bread and margarine with a pot of tea. For the middle classes there would be a cooked breakfast, with cereals and eggs. For the rich a large spread would be laid out, with a choice of dishes such as devilled kidneys or smoked haddock.

Working people ate their main meal at lunchtime or in the early evening. The poor could rarely afford meat, and when they did it was often little more than a thin, fatty stew. Smoked herrings or

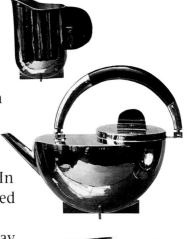

kippers were widely eaten. The diet often did not provide enough nourishment, and many children suffered from **malnutrition**. Diseases such as **rickets** were common.

In a middle class home, lunch might be tinned soup, meat or fish served with vegetables, and a milk pudding or sponge for dessert. There was sometimes a meal mid-afternoon, as well. In Britain, 'tea' included sandwiches, cakes and biscuits. In Germany, coffee and cream would be served with rich cakes or tarts.

For the wealthy, the main meal of the day was dinner. It was served at 8.30 or 9.00 at night, and people often changed into evening dress for it. A gong was sounded to tell the family and their guests that the meal was ready. The servants would bring at least five courses. Dishes would include soup, fish, meat and vegetables, salads, desserts such as **sorbet** or **meringue**, and either cheese or **savoury** specialities served on toast.

After dinner, the men would often remain together. They might drink port or brandy, or play billiards, while the women went into the drawing room to drink tea or coffee, and to talk amongst themselves.

△ Tableware and cutlery took on a new look in the 1920s. This tea service was designed in Germany.

▷ A German film of the early 1920s shows wealthy people dining in style at a public banquet. The table is lavishly decorated and the waiters and servants wear uniform, or 'livery'.

▷ A late-night cup of coffee, as painted by the American artist Edward Hopper in *Nighthawk*s, 1942.

△ Women in a New York bar toast the end of the ban on drinking in 1933. The selling of alcoholic drinks in bars had been illegal for 13 years.

Cocktails – and speakeasies

The fashionable drinks of the 1920s and 1930s were **cocktails**, in which fruit juices or vermouths were mixed with spirits such as gin, whisky or brandy. They were shaken by the bartender and often chilled with ice. A favourite party drink for the rich was champagne, the finest of French sparkling wines.

In the United States, between 1920 and 1933, it was illegal to make or to sell alcoholic drinks. However, secret bars and drinking clubs grew up. They were known as **speakeasies** and they sold smuggled or 'bootlegged' liquor.

Where did people eat out between the wars? The cheapest food, then as now, was to be bought at street stalls or small cafés. Unlike today, the snacks varied greatly from one country to another. Sausages were popular in Germany, herrings in the Netherlands, fish and chips in Britain and hot dogs or doughnuts in the United States.

Meals could be bought at small restaurants and inns, at French *bistros* or German *Gasthäuser*. Restaurant chains which provided lunch for office workers were beginning to appear in cities. In London a Lyons Corner House that opened in 1933 had a staff of 1000. In the United States there were chains of **drugstores** and small eating places called diners, because they were often no bigger than the restaurant car on a train.

The 1926 edition of the *Encyclopaedia Britannica* said that the world's best food and wine were French. Few people would have disagreed. French was the language of cookery and menus were printed in French. The fashionable hotels of Paris or the south of France employed whole armies of under-chefs, chefs, waiters, carvers and *sommeliers*.

Choice or **gourmet** dishes included oysters in season, **caviare**, fillet of sole served with **roes**, trout, partridge, or beef in red wine.

Desserts were often served flambé – soaked in liquor and set aflame. These included pancakes such as *crêpes suzettes* and a flaming ice or *bombe Nero*, invented by the famous French chef Auguste Escoffier (1847-1935).

Some restaurants had musicians and dance floors, or **cabaret** acts to entertain the diners.

△ Today in many cheaper cafés and restaurants people serve themselves. In the 1920s and 30s a uniformed waitress brought the food to the tables. Waitresses for Lyons, London's most famous chain of popular restaurants, were called 'nippies'.

△ A chef checks the dishes before dinner is served, at the Carlton Hotel in the southern French resort of Cannes.

◁ A famous restaurant in Paris, at about the time of the First World War. Guests are arriving in formal dress.

Food for travellers

This was the age when people travelled more than ever before. Those who could afford to buy a motor car drove out into the countryside or to the seaside. Rail was still the more usual method of travelling long distances. Groups of city dwellers would take a train out to the sea, or to the hills and fields for a weekend of hiking.

People on the move needed food that could be carried easily. Picnics were very popular. Picnic food might include fruit, sandwiches,

▷ People who could not afford to buy a car could still have a day out in the country or on the beach by joining a bus or coach party. And no trip was complete without a picnic!

PICNICS.
TAKE THE MOTOR-BUS
FOR PICNICING.

C·R·W·NEVINSON

△ Scouting and Guiding became very popular around the world between the wars. For many children, going to camp was the first time they stayed away from home. They would learn to light campfires and cook up bully beef or bake dough. Older scouts are the cooks at this Christmas camp in Australia in 1939.

△ No meal and no journey was complete without a cigarette. Cigarettes were now smoked by women as well as men. Many advertisements actually claimed that cigarettes were good for the throat! In reality, many of the young smokers of the 1920s and 30s later died of lung cancer and other diseases caused by smoking.

hard-boiled eggs, biscuits and chocolate. Soft drinks varied from one country to another. Root beer or colas were popular in the United States, fizzy lemonade or ginger beer in Britain. Adults drank tea or coffee which was kept hot in **vacuum flasks**. These flasks were first made before the First World War, but the early flasks were difficult to make and were easily broken.

Not all picnics were simple meals. Film stars or rich racegoers might bring along chilled champagne, with baskets or **hampers** of cold chicken and strawberries and cream.

At the seaside, everybody wanted to eat an ice-cream. These were now mostly factory-made and sold on the streets.

Before the age of popular motoring, eating places were found in village and town centres. Now, new cafés and restaurants sprang up along the roadsides, at important junctions or near filling stations. Drivers would stop off for tea, coffee or a snack. This is now taken for granted, but at the time it was something new and exciting.

▽ Sweets and chocolate bars were now factory-made and widely advertised. They could be bought at railway or bus stations and chewed during the journey. Too many sweets often resulted in bad tooth decay.

◁ Sweet wrappers and chocolate boxes often featured the latest aircraft or express trains. International travel was seen as romantic and exciting.

△ A cook on the Baltimore and Ohio Railroad, in the 1920s, carves a turkey in the train's galley.

▽ An air hostess serves coffee on board an American aeroplane. Cabin crew had to serve hot food and drinks without the help of modern microwave ovens.

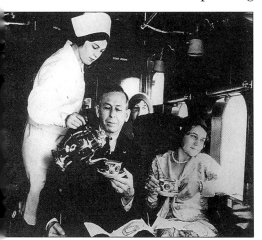

Air travel marked out the years between the wars as a new age. There were now flying boats, large passenger planes which could land on water. An air trip from Britain to Australia took two weeks, while a sea voyage still took six weeks. Planes were not the only aircraft. Long, rigid balloons called airships were popular, until they were found to be unsafe. These could carry a large number of passengers. One German airship carried 117 people across the Atlantic Ocean.

A long trip, such as the one to Australia, included many refuelling stops, where passengers could break their journey, eat and sleep. The first air stewardesses were American. Later air stewardesses travelled on European flights as well. On long-haul flights, they cooked meals in the kitchen, or **galley**, of the plane for the passengers. There were no ready-prepared meals, as there are nowadays.

Most people still travelled overseas by ship. On the ocean-going liners, passengers ate as well as in the best city restaurants. Cruise ships would take holidaymakers around sunny coasts, such as the Mediterranean, and sometimes call in at ports where passengers could eat ashore.

Rich westerners often continued to wear formal dress for dinner in the sweltering heat of India or Africa. This must have amused the local people, who were more sensibly dressed in cool clothes.

▽ Good food was part of the reason for travelling on a big liner. The dining rooms were beautifully decorated. This was the first-class dining-room on the liner *Normandie*.

This dinner was offered to passengers travelling to South Africa from Europe in June 1936:

R.M.S. "LANCASTRIA"   Thursday, June 25, 1936

Dinner

Mixed Fruit Cocktails   Tomato Juice Cocktails
Clam Juice Cocktails   Seville Olives
Salted Almonds   Roasted Peanuts
Radishes
Hors d'Oeuvres, variés

———

(Cold) Tomato Bouillon
Consommé Trois Couleurs   Crême Bonvalet

———

Poached Bream, Boistelle
Fillets of Sole, Meunière

———

Tête de Veau en Tortue
Côtelettes d'Agneau, Clamart
Croquettes de Volaille, Macédoine

———

Prime Ribs and Sirloin of Beef au Jus
Roast Quarters of Lamb, Mint Sauce

———

French Beans   New Carrots in Cream
Corn on the Cob   Vegetable Marrow au Parmesan
Boiled, Roast and Dauphine Potatoes

———

Sorbet au Menthe

———

Roast Norfolk Turkey, Cranberry Sauce

———

Pouding Soufflé Opéra   Peach Sundae
Bavarois d'Amandes   Petits Fours
Vanilla, Lemon and Strawberry Ice-cream and
Wafers

———

Fresh Fruit   Almonds and Raisins   Assorted Nuts
Coffee

Passengers on Special Diet are especially invited to make known
their requirements to the Head Waiter.

Recipes of the 1920s and 30s

Here are some recipes from the 1920s and 1930s that you, your family and friends could eat today. Ask an adult for help when you plan the meals and start to prepare the food.

> **WARNING:** Sharp knives and boiling liquids are dangerous. Hot ovens and pans can burn you. *Always ask an adult to help you* when you are preparing or cooking food in the kitchen.

A cookbook of the 1920s suggests that peanut cookies were ideal for the 'lunch box' that American children took to school. The lunch box might also have included sandwiches of brown bread and cream cheese and an orange.

Peanut cookies

Ingredients

175 g (6 oz) plain white flour

$1/_2$ tsp salt

10 ml (2 tsp) baking powder

100 g (4 oz) sugar

75 g (3 oz) butter or margarine

1 egg

50 ml (2 fl oz) milk

2 tsp lemon juice

100 g (4 oz) chopped peanuts

1. Ask an adult to set the oven to 190°C (375°F).
2. If you are using a lemon, rather than bottled lemon juice, use a lemon squeezer to get the juice out of the lemon.
3. Use a fork to beat the egg in a small bowl.
4. Sift the flour, salt and baking powder into a mixing bowl. Add the sugar.
5. Cut the butter or margarine into small pieces and, using your fingers, rub it into the flour. The mixture should look like fresh breadcrumbs.
6. Stir in the beaten egg, milk and lemon juice. Mix to a dough. Add the chopped peanuts and mix again.
7. Lightly grease the baking tray with a little butter or margarine.
8. Take heaped spoonfuls of the dough and roll into balls. (You should have enough dough for about 24 cookies). Place the balls of dough on to the greased baking tray and press them down lightly with the palm of your hand.

Equipment

lemon squeezer
fork
small bowl
scales
measuring jug
sieve
mixing bowl
wooden spoon
baking tray

Ask an adult to help you when you start to cook.

Hot ovens are dangerous.

9. Ask an adult to place the cookies in the oven in batches and to take them out again after 15 minutes.

Simple dishes like this hotpot were made in country kitchens when meat was scarce. They were also popular between the wars with vegetarians.

Country hotpot

Ingredients

2 leeks

8 medium-sized potatoes

100 g (4 oz) grated cheese

200 ml (7 fl oz) milk

50 g (2 oz) butter

salt and pepper

1. Ask an adult to set the oven to 190°C (375°F).
2. Trim the leeks and split them down the centre with a sharp knife, taking care to keep your fingers out of the way of the blade. Wash the leeks under cold running water. Cut the leeks into short lengths and shred finely.
3. Scrub or peel the potatoes and slice them very finely.
4. Grease an ovenproof dish with a little of the butter. Arrange the leeks and potatoes in layers, sprinkling each layer with salt and pepper as you go.
5. Pour the milk over the top. Add the grated cheese and dot with small pieces of butter.
6. Cover the dish with a lid. Ask an adult to place the dish in the oven and remove it after an hour.

Equipment

sharp knife

grater

scales

measuring jug

bowl

ovenproof dish with lid

Ask an adult to help you when you start to cook.

Hot liquids, sharp knives and ovens are dangerous.

Today people buy most soft drinks ready-mixed in bottles or cans. In the 1920s and 30s people often made their own soft drinks.

Home-made lemonade

Ingredients

2 lemons

25 g (1 oz) sugar

600 ml (1 pt) boiling water

Ask an adult to help you when you start to cook.

1. Wash the lemons and grate off some of the rind.
2. Peel the lemons and cut the fruit into thin slices, taking care to keep your fingers away from the blade of the knife.
3. Place the fruit, rind and sugar in a heat-proof jug and ask an adult to add the boiling water.
4. Leave the lemonade until it is cool. Pour the mixture through a sieve or strainer to remove the rind, pips and fruit.
5. Serve the lemonade in a serving jug.

Equipment

grater

sharp knife

heatproof jug

scales

sieve or strainer

serving jug

Hot liquids and sharp knives are dangerous.

Kedgeree was a British version of an Indian dish called *khicari*. It would be served in a silver dish for breakfast, in the large country houses of the wealthy.

Ingredients

700 ml (1¼ pt) water

675 g (1½ lb) smoked haddock or cod fillets

3 eggs

1 small onion

75 g (3 oz) butter

5 ml (1 tsp) curry powder

350 g (12 oz) long grain rice

45 ml (3 tbs) freshly chopped parsley

1 tbs lemon juice

pepper

salt

Kedgeree

1. Pour the water into a large saucepan and ask an adult to cook the fish in it for you. Once the fish has cooked, leave it to cool for 5 minutes. Ask an adult to take the fish out of the water with a fish slice. Keep both the liquid and the fish on one side.
2. Ask an adult to hard boil the eggs for you. Once they have cooked, leave them to cool.
3. Peel the onion, and chop it into small pieces. Heat the butter in another saucepan and fry the onion with the curry powder for 2 or 3 minutes. Next add the saved fishy water and the rice.
4. Bring the mixture to the boil, then cover it with a lid and cook for 15 minutes until the rice is cooked. Do not stir the mixture until the end of the cooking time.
5. While the rice is cooking, remove all the skin and bones from the cooked fish and flake it. Peel and chop the hard-boiled eggs. Chop the parsley finely.
6. If you are using a lemon, rather than bottled lemon juice, use a lemon squeezer to get the juice out of the lemon.
7. Add the fish to the cooked rice with the eggs, parsley and lemon juice. Mix them all together. Add salt and pepper to taste. Then spoon into a serving dish.

Equipment

2 large saucepans with lids

fish slice

scales

sharp knife

lemon squeezer

serving dish

Ask an adult to help you when you start to cook.

Hot liquids and sharp knives are dangerous.

American chocolate muffins

1. Ask an adult to set the oven to 200°C (400°F).
2. Sift the flour, baking powder and salt into a mixing bowl. Add the sugar and mix well.
3. Make a well in the centre and add the eggs and milk. Mix thoroughly. Next mix in the grated chocolate.

Ingredients

350 g (12 oz) plain white flour

3 tsp baking powder

50 g (2 oz) sugar

½ tsp salt

2 eggs

200 ml (7 fl oz) milk

100 g (4 oz) butter

50 g (2 oz) grated plain chocolate

Equipment

mixing bowl

scales

sieve

wooden spoon

grater

deep bun tray

Ask an adult to help you when you start to cook.

Hot ovens are dangerous.

4. Grease a deep bun tray with a little butter or margarine. Spoon some of the mixture into each compartment on the bun tray so that each hollow is half full.
5. Ask an adult to place the muffins in the oven and take them out after 20 minutes when they are cooked.

This salad takes its name from the famous Waldorf-Astoria hotel in New York City.

Waldorf Salad

Ingredients

4 red eating apples

30 ml (2 tbs) lemon juice

5 ml (1 tsp) caster sugar

120 ml (8 tbs) mayonnaise

4 sticks of celery

50 g (2 oz) shelled walnuts

1 crisp lettuce

Equipment

sharp knife

scales

small bowl

lemon squeezer

fork

measuring jug

mixing bowl

salad bowl

Sharp knives are dangerous.

1. Wash the apples. Chop each one in half, taking care to keep your fingers away from the blade of the knife. Carefully remove the apple cores. Cut two apple halves into neat slices, and chop the rest into small cubes.
2. If you are using a lemon, rather than bottled lemon juice, use a lemon squeezer to get the juice out of the lemon.
3. Make a dressing in a mixing bowl by mixing together the lemon juice, caster sugar and one tablespoon of the mayonnaise.
4. Dip the apple slices in the dressing, remove them and keep them on one side.
5. Put the apple cubes in the dressing and leave them for 30 minutes.
6. Wash the celery sticks, and cut them into short lengths.
7. Chop the shelled walnuts into small pieces.
8. Add the chopped celery, walnuts and the rest of the mayonnaise to the apple cubes in the dressing. Mix them all together thoroughly.
9. Pull the leaves from the lettuce, wash them and leave them to dry. Put the clean, dry leaves into a salad bowl and make a nest.
10. Put the mixture of celery, walnuts, apple cubes and dressing into the nest of lettuce leaves.
11. Decorate the top of the salad with a layer of apple slices.

Glossary

blancmange: Milk mixed with cornflour, gelatine and flavouring, to make a mould or jelly.

brand name: The name given by a producer to their product to help to distinguish it from other products of the same kind, e.g. tomato sauce.

cabaret: Musical or other entertainment put on in a restaurant or nightclub.

caviare: The eggs of a fish called the sturgeon.

cereal: 1. Any grain crop, such as wheat, rice or millet.
2. Any breakfast food made from grain.

cocktail: An alcoholic drink – usually made by mixing different kinds of spirits.

colonist: One of a group of people who settle in another country.

combine harvester: A moving machine which cuts the stalks and removes the seeds from crops such as wheat.

cure: To preserve meat by salting or drying.

dessert: A sweet dish or pudding.

dresser: A sideboard with shelves and drawers for storing crockery, pots and pans.

drugstore: In the United States, a shop which sells light meals and soft drinks as well as pills, soap, etc.

essence: A concentrated liquid, often made from a foodstuff which can be mixed with water for drinking.

export: To send produce for sale to another country.

famine: A time when people starve because there is not enough food.

fertilizer: A natural substance or a chemical used to enrich the soil.

freight: Goods carried from one place to another.

galley: The kitchen on a ship, aircraft or train.

gourmet: Somebody who knows about and enjoys eating good food.

hamper: A large wicker basket used for carrying food.

kipper: 1. To preserve a fish by salting, drying and smoking.
2. A fish that has been preserved in this way.

kitchen range: A stove heated by solid fuel. Food was cooked over the fire, or in the ovens at the side of the fire.

larder: A small room or cupboard, used for storing food.

malnutrition: The effect of either not eating enough food, or not eating the right kind of food.

meringue: A very light mixture of sugar and egg white, baked in the oven to make a sweet crust or topping.

migrant farmworkers: People who travel from one farm to another in search of temporary work.

pantry: A small room used for the storage of food, or plates, glasses and cutlery.

pasteurised: Heat-treated to kill germs. The treatment was worked out by the French scientist Louis Pasteur in 1857. Dairies began to pasteurise milk in 1907 but it was many years before it became common practice.

pest:	Any creature which destroys or damages crops.
pesticide:	A natural substance or chemical, used to kill pests.
poacher:	Someone who takes or kills animals, birds or fish, without permission, on someone else's land.
prairies:	The grasslands of North America.
pump:	A machine to raise, extract or boost the flow of water.
refrigerated transport:	Ships or trucks in which food remains frozen during the journey.
rickets:	A disease caused by poor diet, in which a child's bones become soft.
roe:	Fishes' eggs.
safe:	A small cupboard in which meat or fish could be kept cool and free from flies.
savoury:	A tasty, non-sweet snack served before or after a meal.
sharecroppers:	Farmers in the United States who paid the rent for their land with a share of the crops they grew.
smallholding:	A very small farm.
***sommelier*:**	In a restaurant, a wine waiter or the person who is in charge of the drinks.
sorbet:	A water ice flavoured with fruit or alcoholic drinks.
speakeasy:	An illegal drinking club or bar.
stainless steel:	A type of steel mixed with chromium so that it stays shiny and doesn't rust.
stockyards:	Enclosures and slaughterhouses to which cattle are sent by rail.
strain:	A group of plants or animals which have been bred from other groups of the same kind to improve their strength or quality.
vacuum flask:	A bottle, with an airless jacket which keeps the contents hot or cold.
yield:	A measure of the quantity of crops grown successfully in a particular area of land. A good harvest gives a high yield.

Further reading

1902-1926, Freda Kelsall, 'How we used to live' series (A & C Black, 1988)

1920s, Margaret Sharman, 'Take Ten Years' series (Evans Brothers Limited, 1991)

The 1920s, Richard Tames, 'Picture History of the 20th Century' series (Franklin Watts, 1991)

The 1920s, Betty Williams, 'Portrait of a Decade' series (Batsford, 1988)

1930s, Ken Hills, 'Take Ten Years' series (Evans Brothers Limited, 1991)

The 1930s, Charles Freeman, 'Portrait of a Decade' series (Batsford, 1988)

The 1930s, Richard Tames, 'Picture History of the 20th Century' series (Franklin Watts, 1991)

The 1930s, Neil Thomson, 'When I was Young' series (Franklin Watts, 1991)

The 1940s, Nance Lui Fyson, 'Portrait of a Decade' series (Batsford, 1988)

Britain in the 1930s, Charles Freeman, 'Living Through History' series (Batsford, 1985)

A Family in the Thirties, Sue Crawford, 'How They Lived' series (Wayland Publishers Limited, 1988)

Young in the twenties, Eleanor Allen (A & C Black, 1988)

Index